OUR RIGHTS

Health

First published in paperback in 2009

Published by Evans Brothers Limited in association with Save the Children UK.

Evans Brothers Limited.
2A Portman Mansions
Chiltern Street
London W1U 6NR

British Library Cataloguing in Publication Data
Duckworth, Katie
    Health. – (Children's rights)
    1. Right to health care – Juvenile literature
    2. Children's rights – Juvenile literature
    I. Title
    323.3'52

ISBN 978 0 237 537739

Printed in China

Credits

Series editor: Louise John
Editor: Nicola Edwards
Designer: Simon Borrough
Production: Jenny Mulvanny

Acknowledgements
Cover: Liba Taylor/Save the Children UK
Title page: Liba Taylor/Save the Children UK
p6: Tim Hetherington
p7: Jenny Matthews/Network
p8: Dan White
p9: Anne Heslop
p10: Jodi Bieber/Network
p11: Jodi Bieber/Network
p12a: Neil Cooper
p12b: Dan White
p13: Kalpesh Lathigra
p14: Brendan Paddy
p15a: Brendan Paddy
p15b: Brendan Paddy
p16: Dan White
p17a: Dan White
p17b: Anne Heslop
p18: Liba Taylor/Save the Children UK
p19a: Tim Hetherington/Network
p19b: Tim Hetherington /Network
p20a: Tim Hetherington/Network
p20b: Dan White
p21: Dan White
p22: Stuart Freedman/Network
p23a: Stuart Freedman/Network
p23b: Stuart Freedman/Network
p24a: Dan White
p24b: Tim Hetherington/Network
p25: Pieternella Pieterse
p26: Tim Hetherington/Network
p27: Tim Hetherington/Network

Contents

All children have rights   6

Children have the right to healthcare   8

Khamis' story   10

Children have the right to good food   12

Fatima's story   14

Children have the right to clean water   16

Abaynesh's story   18

Children have the right to
health education   20

Ana Catalina's story   22

Children have the right to protect
themselves against HIV and AIDS   24

Gillian and Bernard's story   26

Glossary   28

Index   29

Further reading and addresses   30

All children have rights

The history of rights for children
In 1919 a remarkable British woman called Eglantyne Jebb founded the Save the Children Fund. She wanted to help children who were dying of hunger as a result of the First World War. Four years later, she wrote a special set of statements, a list of children's rights. Eglantyne Jebb said that her aim was "to claim certain rights for children and labour for their universal recognition". This meant that she wanted agreement throughout the world on children's rights.

It was many years before countries around the world agreed that children have rights, but eventually the statements became recognised in international law in 1989. They are known as the United Nations Convention on the Rights of the Child (UNCRC). The rights in the UNCRC are based on the idea that everyone deserves fair treatment.

The UNCRC protects the rights of children around the world to a happy, healthy and secure childhood.

The UNCRC is a very important document. Almost every country in the world has signed it, so it relates to most of the world's children. The rights listed in the UNCRC cover all areas of children's lives such as their right to have a home and their right to be educated.

Rights for all?
The UNCRC should mean that the rights of children everywhere are guaranteed. However, this is not the case. Every day, millions of children are denied their rights. Children in many countries suffer discrimination because they are poor, or disabled, or because they work for a living. It might be because of their religion or race, or whether they are a boy or a girl.

Children are very vulnerable, so they need special care and protection. The UNCRC exists to try to make sure that they are cared for and protected.

The right to good health

The convention is a list of 54 Articles. Some of the Articles in the UNCRC are about every child's right to good health. The most important one is Article 24. It says:

"You have the right to the best health possible and to medical care and information that will help you to stay well."

But despite what Article 24 says, every year around 10 million children around the world die from preventable diseases.

Save the Children

Save the Children UK is part of the International Save the Children Alliance, working in over 100 countries worldwide to make children's rights a reality. This book and the others in the series tell the stories of children around the world who are achieving their rights with the help of Save the Children projects.

This boy's right to be healthy and receive good healthcare is at risk, because his family is poor and he has to work for a living.

Children have the right to healthcare

Rights for all   Children everywhere have the right to good healthcare. All children are entitled to the advice, medicines and other treatment they need to be healthy. Unfortunately, many children do not get the healthcare that is their right. Around the world millions of children die from serious illnesses such as malaria and pneumonia.

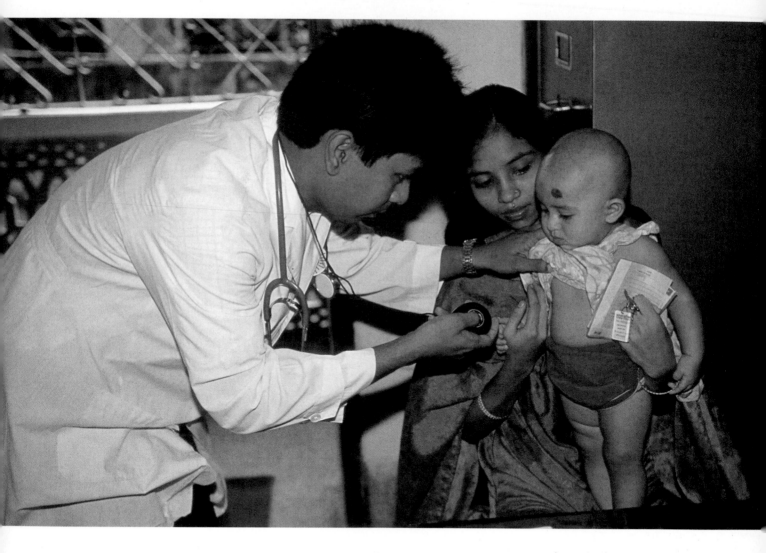

Poor and unhealthy   Many developing countries do not have enough money to provide free health services like the UK's National Health Service, so they charge for medicines or visits to a doctor. But parents may be too poor to afford even a few pence for medicine. Or they may have to use up their life savings or sell precious animals to pay for healthcare for their children.

Tamana lives in Bangladesh. She is being vaccinated against childhood diseases at a health clinic.

DID YOU KNOW?

Half of all the families in Africa live on less than 66 pence a day.

A long wait

In many poor countries there are not enough hospitals and clinics or trained doctors and nurses. If a child falls ill, a mother might walk miles to the clinic, only to find that the medicines she needs are not available. Heile is from Ethiopia, in Africa. The nearest doctor is 20 miles away from Heile's house. When he visits the doctor he has to wait for six hours.

In a disaster such as an earthquake, children have a right to the healthcare they need, but it is not always available.

Good healthcare

Many children living in poor countries dream of becoming a doctor or a nurse because they realise how important healthcare is to them and their communities. All over the world, children want healthcare to be available to them near to where they live. They want health centres and hospitals run by trained workers and all the medicines they need, at a price their parents can afford.

"They say money makes it possible to stay healthy. Rich and poor people should be offered the same help because they are all human beings." Rosa, 13, Guatemala

9

Khamis' story

Khamis stood up to his knees in the pale blue sea. His kanga, the traditional cloth worn by boys in his Zanzibar village, stuck to his hot skin. It felt deliciously cool in the scorching morning sun. Khamis peered across the horizon, searching for fishing boats returning from their daily catch. Nothing. Perhaps it was too early.

Or perhaps he just couldn't see them. Three months ago, he had caught an infection from playing in stagnant water. His eyes were stinging and sore and sometimes his sight was so fuzzy he could hardly see. Now of course, he knew better than to play in dirty water. His teacher had told him it was dangerous, but it was too late now.

Khamis splashed back under the water. Soon tiny dots on the horizon turned into boats ploughing their way to shore. Other local boys appeared as if from nowhere. If they helped unload the slithery silver fish and heaved them to market for the fishermen they could each earn a fish. It was worth the mad scramble to get to the boats and the fishy smell that stayed on their fingers all day.

A few hours later, Khamis walked home and added his payment to the meal of fried fish and rice his mum was cooking. Khamis was happy to contribute the fish, but he wished there was a bit more money to go around in his family. Then he could get the medicine he needed to make his eyes better. The eye drops from the village clinic hadn't been enough to cure the infection. Khamis would have to visit a bigger clinic, which was miles away from his home.

There was so much he would like to change about life in Kijini village! If Khamis were president he would make sure that the health centre was piled high with medicines cheap enough for everyone to afford. There would be more doctors and all the village children would go to school.

In his ideal world, Khamis and his friends would no longer have to work.

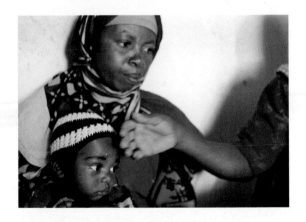

The clinic in the small village where Khamis lives stocks only very basic medicines. Save the Children is helping to train nurses and other clinic staff to improve the healthcare of the children of Zanzibar.

Children have the right to good food

This plane is bringing emergency food aid to hungry families in Sudan. It is important for families to receive the kind of basic foods they would normally eat.

Your rights   Plenty of good food helps make you fit and healthy. Not enough food, or too much unhealthy food, makes you ill.

All children have the right to enough healthy food. But even though there is enough food in the world to feed everyone, millions of children go hungry because their families have no way of getting the food they need. They may be too poor to buy food or unable to produce enough food from their land.

Food for life   Children have to eat to be healthy. Food provides all the nutrients we need to feel well, but we need a mixture of foods. This is why adults want children to have a balanced diet.

These children live on the streets of Vietnam. Save the Children supports a project that helps them get food.

Problems   Around the world, more than 150 million children are denied the right to enough food to keep them healthy. Children who do not eat enough food or who eat the same poor food every day develop malnutrition. This makes them tired and weak. They struggle to concentrate in school and catch infections and diseases.

Most of these children live in developing countries, but not all do. One third of all the children in the world under the age of five are malnourished. Children from families on low incomes in the UK can develop malnutrition because they eat an unhealthy diet.

Famine   You may have seen images on television of children during times of famine with large round stomachs. These children are very malnourished and could die of starvation. Luckily, famine is not very common. At times of famine in countries such as Ethiopia and Sudan, international aid agencies give out emergency food aid to families.

Solutions   There are many things which can be done to make sure children have enough food to eat before a crisis happens. Save the Children discusses with governments how to plan for and prevent emergencies occurring. It runs projects to help families to help themselves, for example by providing nets and rods for fishing, or helping families to set up small businesses.

A cow not only provides a family with nutritious milk, it can also be used to prepare land for growing food.

Fatima's story

Fatima is 12 years old. She comes from Afghanistan, one of the poorest countries in the world. She used to love her old life in the village of Chor Baluk. The countryside was green and fertile, and there were trees and a running stream. Her dad was a successful farmer. He made sure that there was plenty of milk and yoghurt, potatoes, rice and meat for his family.

But gradually, after a few seasons without rain, the stream dried up and the crops no longer flourished. Fatima could remember the terrible day her dad decided to sell first their camel, then their horse, cow and donkey, to get money for food. Without the animals there was no more milk or meat and no way of doing heavy farm work. In a time of drought, without rain, it was impossible for her dad to grow enough food. The whole family began to go hungry.

Fatima misses home. She would like her family to produce food on their own land.

Worse was to come. Fatima's village was attacked by soldiers working for the rulers of Afghanistan. The family's home was destroyed. Fatima and her family were forced to leave and trek hundreds of miles to a camp in Mazar-i-Sharif. It was crowded with thousands of other families fleeing drought and war. Fatima's dad hoped to find work, perhaps as a porter at the local market, but day after day he returned to his family without a job.

Aid agencies made sure they got basic foods and Fatima's mum did what she could with the oil, beans, and flour for bread. But it was not easy to live on so little. Fatima grew bored of the same food day in, day out and her mum worried about her children's health.

There were some good things about life at the camp. Fatima made friends with the other girls, and nurses at the health centre looked after her when she was ill. But the whole family dreamed of a time when they could go back to Chor Baluk and farm the land once more. They just needed to know they would be safe, and of course to have the all-important rain. Then they would return home as fast as they could and prepare their land to grow crops.

"I was sad when I first saw the camp," says Fatima. "There was no water for heating or cooking. We were hungry and there was no food."

Fatima and her brothers Farema and Nesah Ahmed, have a right to good food to keep them healthy. Aid agencies are helping to provide food and health services in camps to families like Fatima's.

15

Children have the right to clean water

Having a supply of clean drinking water is essential for good health.

"Every house should have clean water to drink." Zarifa, 12, India

Wonderful water   People need to drink water just to stay alive. We need it to keep us clean, and we need it to grow food so we get enough to eat. Without enough water it is difficult to stay healthy. Water is a basic human need and we all have a right to it.

Clean water   It is important that water is safe to drink. Clean water is essential so that we do not catch illnesses from it, such as diarrhoea which is caused by parasites getting into water supplies. Diarrhoea kills over 2 million children every year worldwide, even though it is completely avoidable.

Not enough water   One thousand million people around the world – that's around 20 times the population of the UK – are denied their right to clean water. Most of these people live in developing countries such as Ethiopia and India, where the hot climate means they need more water, not less. In some countries, including the UK, some families have to use water meters. Saving money by cutting down on how much water they use can put the health of their children at risk.

DID YOU KNOW?
Every eight seconds a child dies of a disease caused by a lack of clean water.

These children enjoy playing in the floodwater but it may be dangerous to their health. Many deadly diseases are caused by dirty water.

Water on tap

In many developing countries children have to walk miles to collect water from streams and rivers. If they are lucky there will be a well or a standpipe near their home. There are taps in only a very few houses.

Water projects

Wells and pipes are the safest way to transport water from place to place, but they have to be kept clean. Families in developing countries where water is not treated understand why sanitation is important. Projects are set up to bring clean water to where it is needed and help families to keep water supplies clean and water systems working.

After a disaster such as an earthquake, safe water for drinking and washing is often in short supply.

Abaynesh's story

Abaynesh lives with her aunt in Ethiopia, in Dedere village. Ethiopia is a hot and dry country. Many poor people find it difficult to get enough water.

There are no water taps in Abaynesh's house so she has to collect water from the village spring. It used to be hard work and the water was dirty until Save the Children laid some concrete to protect the spring from animals and put in four new taps for the spring water to flow through. Abaynesh tells her story:

"In the past, I used to come to the spring four times a day. I collected five litres each time, and we used the water for drinking, preparing food and cleaning.

"The water tasted bad. It was dirty and smelly. The water was very bad, because people and many animals like dogs and donkeys used to drink here. It was also very crowded. There were maybe ten or 15 people together at one time. We used to stay for a long time to collect the water – maybe an hour. Sometimes people pushed me away when we were queuing.

Abaynesh is healthier and happier now that the village spring is protected and the community knows how to look after it.

"Now things are much better. It only takes ten minutes to take the water home. Now we can use four taps, so it makes things easier. We just stand on the platform, open the tap, and wait for the water to fill the pot.

"The water is clear and clean. We notice the difference, and we laugh, because we remember that the previous spring was really dirty.

"Because collecting water takes less time, we can help our parents in other ways – like working in the house, cleaning the pans and plates, and washing clothes. We also have more time to study. Before, when our school was in the morning and our parents sent us to collect the water, we were late and we missed the classes.

"We are very proud of our spring because we know that it protects us from water diseases. We are really happy to look after it."

New taps like these bring clean water to Dedere and other villages in Ethiopia.

Abaynesh now has lots more time to help out around the house, go to school and play with her friends.

"I like working with other children because you can share things."

Sarah, 10, Uganda

Children's clubs

Children have the right to have their say about their own health and to find out how to stay fit and healthy. In poorer parts of the world, some children belong to special clubs where they find out how to take care of their health. They might learn about healthy eating or how to keep toilets and water supplies clean. The illnesses children learn about can be very dangerous, so the club leaders make sure they get the important information across with games, drama and songs.

Some club members become peer educators. This means that they teach other children, and even their parents, what they have learned. It makes children feel great to take responsibility for their own health and the health of others in their communities.

At the club she goes to in Uganda, Sarah has learned how to protect herself against AIDS.

Poor children like these boys from Cambodia have a right to find out how to take care of their health.

Healthy changes

Educating children about their health helps to prevent illnesses and disease. For example, malaria kills millions of children around the world. Malaria is caused by mosquitoes living in stagnant water. Children who have learned the cause of malaria are much more likely to encourage their communities to clear away stagnant water and not to play near mosquito breeding grounds.

Children at risk

Children who have to live in difficult circumstances, such as street children and refugees, often have health problems. Tamir is a homeless boy from Mongolia. He lives in crowded conditions in the city. Many of his friends have tuberculosis, a dangerous disease. Tamir belongs to a club where he learns how to avoid diseases such as tuberculosis.

In poor parts of the world, HIV, the virus that causes AIDS, is also spreading quickly among young people. Children have the right to learn how to avoid catching the virus. You can read more about children living with AIDS on pages 24 and 25.

These girls have learned that washing their hands carefully helps to prevent the spread of infectious diseases.

DID YOU KNOW?

Malaria kills 3,000 children in Africa every day.

21

Ana Catalina's story

Twelve-year-old Ana Catalina felt as if her head was going to burst! As she pushed open the door of the sweltering bakery, the cold evening air gave her an icy punch that almost knocked her over. It took her a few seconds to catch her breath. She wrapped her bright Mayan scarf over her head and strode shivering up the dusty street to her house.

Ana Catalina didn't mind working in the bakery. In fact, she liked it. It kept her out of her parents' overcrowded house. But most importantly, her wages paid for her to go to evening school.

However, her face broke into a grin at the thought that today was Friday. No work for two whole days! Hurrah! It was school on Saturday and then on Sunday she would go to the girls' club. She could chat and enjoy herself with her friends, other girls who also worked in Guatemala City, in Guatemala, Central America.

The club had made a real difference to her life. In the past few years, she had learned to read and write and how to make traditional Mayan handicrafts to sell. Last week they had all discussed how to keep healthy. She had learned so much about taking care of herself and had a million and one questions for the girl who had introduced herself as a health promoter.

Ana Catalina's family are indigenous Mayan people. Mayans can't always find or afford good healthcare so education is important.

Ana Catalina's club is supported by Save the Children. The girls there enjoy learning about how to prevent illness.

Ana Catalina works 11 hours a day in her aunt's tortilla factory. "I never thought that one day I'd be able to learn about my rights," she says.

Her mum greeted her at the door of her house with a hug. She looked pale after her long day behind the counter of the family shoe shop. It was a shame that her mum had to work so hard, but at least Ana Catalina didn't have to ask her for money any more. Two years ago, her dad had sold some of his land to pay for a stomach operation she needed. Healthcare was so expensive for poor families like hers, and it hadn't even been completely successful.

Perhaps on Sunday at the girls' club she would discover how to sort out her health problems once and for all.

Children have the right to protect themselves against HIV and AIDS

AIDS is a killer The HIV virus attacks the body and makes it unable to fight off any disease. HIV, which causes AIDS, is spread when blood or other bodily fluids from an infected person mix with another person's. Poverty and AIDS are closely linked. In poor parts of the world, where people are less able to afford medicine and healthcare, HIV is spreading with terrible speed. AIDS affects millions of children: one or both of their parents may have died of AIDS, or they may have become infected with HIV themselves.

In this school in Vietnam, children who have been trained as peer educators teach their classmates about HIV and AIDS.

The need for protection Children whose parents have died of AIDS need a lot of help. They are often very poor, and have no one to look after them. Some of these children also have to care for their younger brothers and sisters. They may also have to deal with the prejudice of other people, who make them feel 'different' and isolated at a time when they most need comfort and help.

Save the Children works with groups which provide services such as mobile health clinics for children whose parents are ill or have died. Other groups train volunteers who travel around villages, spreading information about HIV and AIDS and helping to overcome prejudice against people who have become infected.

"Children should be given more information, both at home and at school."

Gillian, 14, Uganda

DID YOU KNOW?

8,500 children become infected with HIV every day.

These children in Tanzania are acting out a play which tells others how to avoid AIDS.

Hafisa and her brother lived on their own for three months after they were orphaned by AIDS. Now the children live with their grandmother.

The need for information There is no cure for AIDS, so preventing it is very important. Children have the right to learn how they can avoid the virus. They need information, presented in a way they can understand. Aid workers have found that it is often children themselves who are best at teaching each other about HIV and AIDS. Many projects around the world train children to pass on information to others. It is information that is urgently needed in the fight against the virus.

Gillian and Bernard's story

Gillian, who is 14, and her younger brother Bernard, 11, live in Arua, in north-west Uganda. The children live with their mother's sister and her family, because their mother, who has HIV, is in hospital. Their father died of an AIDS-related illness when the children were little. Bernard says:

"Our mother's health is always up and down. Sometimes she gets better; sometimes she's sick. At the moment she's very ill, and when we see her we feel very scared because she's staying in the hospital longer than normal, and she seems to be sicker than ever before."

Gillian and Bernard holding their books which help them share stories and ideas with their sick mother.

Although Gillian and Bernard's mother is seriously ill, she has found a way to help her children to understand her illness. At the same time she has shown them how they can hold on to their memories of her. For each child she has prepared a 'memory book'. Along with photographs, this contains her memories of the children when they were younger and the special times they shared. In the book, she gives the children her thoughts and advice about their lives now and her hopes for their health and happiness in the future.

In Uganda, the idea that mothers living with AIDS could create memory books for their children was developed by a group supported by Save the Children. Having a memory book from their mother has helped Bernard and Gillian know more about their own history. Bernard explains:

"I like the memory book because our mother told us about our clan and her memories of the past. Now we know things that we didn't know before, like our family history."

Through the book, their mother has helped them to understand more about HIV and AIDS. Gillian says:

Support groups in Uganda help children living with AIDS like Gillian and Bernard. Maicheal, whose mother has HIV, is learning to be a tailor so that he can earn money to live on.

"With the memory book I'm a bit more prepared, and I know what will happen if she dies." Bernard agrees. He says: "I wouldn't know about AIDS if it hadn't been for this book."